Postponing the Crone

Azalea Ælfric

Azalea Ælfric

Copyright © 2012 Author Name

All rights reserved.

ISBN: 1508685789
ISBN-13: 9781508685784

DEDICATION

To my Dionysus without whom I would have frozen

CONTENTS

Acknowledgments	i
Postponing The Crone	3
My Own Dionysus	4
What Use These Damned Fairytales	5
Questions and Answers	6
On Knowing	8
Unnameable	10
Fairytale Ending	11
Circuit	12
Blind or Drunk	14
Have A Good Day	15
Your Album	16
The Flying Sofa	17
To Keep	18
Nine Lives	20
Connected	22
Fortune's Turn	23
A Life Less Hurried	24

The Fan Of You	26
Dionysus and Aphrodite's Fall	28
Shrew No More	29
Resolve	30
Ode To My Pubic Hair And Its Lack Thereof	32
British	34
Holiday Forecast	35
Humble Pie	36
Before You Go	38
Excluded No More	40
Birds Of Paradise	41
Questions For The New Year	42
My Modern Hero	44
Sweet Dreams	46
The Wolves	48
Song Interrupted	49
Man-Hole	50
Telescope	51
Larder Full of Love	52

With thanks to Emma and Simon for their introduction to the Honey of Love; to Barbara, Ruth and Karin for taking me to Womad; to Freya and Sara for Painting My Nails on the night that counted; and to Jess for her expertise on the highs and lows of Love. To Ginny for introducing me to Anastasia and to Sarah for deepening and broadening my acquaintance with her, and to Lana for also knowing what it is like to 'Scream like a Spring Cat'.

> "The lunatic, the lover and the poet,
> Are of imagination all compact"
>
> (A Midsummer Night's Dream; Act 5, Scene 1)

Postponing The Crone

She came for me in the night
Whipping me into her sweat
Without reasonable reason
Whitening my blonde
Without bringing wisdom
Widening my curves
Without mercy

I lay down
Washed up on her shores
Thirsting to death
And I wept

When up you sailed buoyant with Ecstasy
Taking my hand and my breast and my breath, and me,
Lifting me up to your sweet clouds of fantasy
Lifting me up on a pillow of dreams

And I parted my lips and a trembling started
There issued a sigh
Then a cry
Then a roar
And she fled through the night
Retreating in fear from me
Seeing me lie with you
Maiden once more.

My Own Dionysus

And was it fate
Or justice
Or some pagan blessing
That up you sailed
To my shores
Where I lay open
Helpless
My armour
Stripped
My wounds
Washed clean
By all those tears

And from my beach
I hear your question
To answer is
To bare my soul
To avoid, invent, or please is
Too hard
I tell you who I am
You do not run

You ask some more
And I ask too
You tell me some
And I like you
You touch my back
And I am gone
Your kiss connects
And we are one

What Use These Damned Fairytales?

The Princess already who knew she was
Before they rescued her from the rain and
Ruined a much needed night's sleep by
Sabotage, before throwing her back out into the
Street for not deigning to complain.

And when she was
Suffocating in a glass coffin
Needing that elusive kiss
They stared impotently at her young beauty
Never thinking to smash the glass and
Let her kiss the frog of her choice.

But now, in a castle overgrown with brambles
Near drowning in Cinderella's chores
Her lover comes from behind, kisses her neck
Caresses her shoulders, her back and beyond.

She picks up her shiny pink shoes and
Finally goes with him to The Ball.

Questions and Answers

'Who Am I', you ask
The woman you have
Just Met
Luckily, she is a mermaid
With underwater vision and
Can swim into the
Depths with you
Diving into salt waters
Plundering the oysters of their
Pearls

'Who Am I', you think
And the woman you have
Just Met
Happily is a sphinx
And intuits that it is not
Your work but the
Mind food of your commute
That fuels you
That it is not
In your Day but in your
Intoxicating Night that you
Shine most brightly

Postponing The Crone

'Where Am I Going?', you do not ask
The woman you have
Just Met
Almost impossibly, she is goddesses and
She will walk in the meadow with you
She will hunt in the night with you
She will talk of constellations with you
And listen to your song
She will tend the fire for you
Warm you and feed you and
Love you
And your kin
Wherever you
Choose

On Knowing

And some may think that I'm too old
And some may think my hopes too bold
And some may think and think again
For what do thoughts beget but pain

For yes I have had years before
The years that grazed and wrenched and tore
But those were prior to meeting you
In your most godly frame

For from your eyes a nectar flows
The sweet liqueur of one who knows
And from your lips a lion's purr
That cause my Lioness to stir

And from your touch both silk and fire
Which glides and licks sparks of desire
And from your skin a musk sublime
Which takes me back through gates of time

And from your heart truth reaches me
And takes us to the honeyed sea
Where nightly we can naked swim
Where stars and salt get drawn within
And sighs and cries are all around
And purest love does full abound

Postponing The Crone

So I
Will dream
And have my spring
And we will fly
On Love's sweet wing
And we
Will shake
And make
And sing
And have
Our youth again

Unnameable

Here in this hollow
Cupped between our skins
Scented with musk
Heat and the hint
Of a familiar flower
Lies the elusive compulsion

Call it Love
A Pocket of Air
A Pull
A Charge
Call it Chi
Call it God
It is of us
And we are
Love

Fairytale Ending

And for all of those years
Trapped in tall towers
Hair getting shorter
With less and less
Prospect
Of a prince
Who would climb all that way up to me

Then
You walked past my brambles
Straight up the steps
And in through my front door
You battered the pea in my mattress
Flat
And now I lie comfortable
Still complex
But no longer
Complicated

Circuit

I felt your charge
Run through our lips
Across my skin
Down to my breast
It travelled lower
To my core
An ache
That I could scarce ignore
It leapt a synapse
Through our skins
Back to your flame
And up again
Your chest
Your cheek
Your sumptuous lips
Which hold me
In a perfect bliss
Your hips, your lips
Where they hold mine
In sweet embrace
A loop divine

Postponing The Crone

Or was it me
That lit your flame
That made you melt
Yet hard again
That led your fingers
To my breast
Then on to where
I love it best
My skin
My kiss
My sweet caress
That eased your ache
And swelled your chest
That drew you deep
Inside of me
To that eternal mystery

Blind or Drunk

What did Bacchus see in Ariadne
There on the beach so wild
Did he see a tear-stained needy waif
Or a mortal to bear his child

Did he see a woman who'd lost her cares
Who was ready to be made divine
What was it that made young Bacchus
Feed sweet Ariadne his wine

Was he blind to the lines
That made trace on her face
Of the cuts that had bled so deep
Or did he see in her breast
The sweet treasure chest
Of a heart that he'd like to keep

Did he know when he spoke
Of the love he'd invoke
From this woman who'd become divine
What made sweet Dionysus
Become the man that's mine?

Have a Good Day

"How dare you tell me what kind of day should have!?"

I hope you have a fruitful day
I hope that knowledge comes your way
I hope you get to weave and flow
And find the things you ready know
I hope you get to stretch your mind
And reach and learn, new wisdom find
I hope your wit you exercise
And feel your inspiration rise
I hope your muscles get to move
Ant stretch and flex and prove their prove
I hope you smile and find some fun
In this one circle of the sun.

Your Album

Firstly the chub of you and those two eyes
Steadily connecting despite your tiny frame

Then toddling, tidily combed
Then teasing your sister in close

Then taller, legs up on stilts
Your own person
Gazelle, or rather
Young stag
Pink cheeks and brown eyes
Alert energised

Then taller still
With comrades camping
The pulling thrust of you
Emerges

That's the end of the album
That your mother made of you

But out from its pages slips
A loose image of adult curls
The dangerous glint of you
I would have been at your mercy
Had we met then but mercifully
Two decades have tamed you and
Here gazing up at your beauty now
I can at least
Just about
Breathe

The Flying Sofa

There in your love den
We played and we laid
With music and massage
Whenever I stayed

Ice cream and 'treats'
You rubbing your hands
Aladdin and Jasmine
All set for strange lands

We flew on your sofa
Ecstatic through skies
Dipping and gliding
Miraculous highs

Landing in fireworks
Then riding again
Buoyant, uplifted on
Love's endless flame

To Keep

And In the stillness of the night
I dream I'm in your bed
I'd feel your heat
Our skin would meet
And I am there instead

I kiss your cheek
And touch your chest
Your belly and your thigh
I turn around
Without a sound
Til you draw out my sigh

You touch me sweet
And venture in
Where silk and sea
Do meet
You seek my pearl
My soft uncurl
The urge to be complete

Your confidence now enters me
And deeper still we dive
The ancient hunt
Inside us both
Urging us alive

Postponing The Crone

And there beyond the rocking tide
The soothing swell and rise
We travel through a mystic gate
And seize our treasured prize

We revel there in wonderment
A symphony of bliss
Soak up the shimmer
And the light
And seal it with a kiss

An envelope of memories
And further promise too
And that is what I keep
And share
In sending this to you

Nine Lives

I am sphinx with nine lives
Or as many as I want
Take stock of stories ready told
Before my face gets gaunt

My first life was pure revelry
On luscious grasses green
Down golden paths, 'mongst fragrant shrubs
Most beauteous garden seen

Slight shift as dusk brought moist of dew
And to my lips first kiss
A foreign boy, exotic tang
And sweet taste of first bliss

Third chapter came with leaving home
And finding feet and food
And learning how to steer my course
Traversing desperate mood

In fourth I went to capital
To learn and search and seek
Ecstatic dance and mystic trance
The highest yet found peak

In fifth stage I did walk on heath
And sing into the wild
Connecting with the earth beneath
And healing inner child

Postponing The Crone

A sunny city brought new life
And new work I created
To stay there I had all my hope
But seems it wasn't fated

Seventh life brought work then love
Then kids and solid roots
But when love ended and began
I put back on my boots

And so this eighth life: what shalt be
More work to grow, then age
Or is there time for one fresh start
Before the final stage

The ninth life will both start and end
But do I want to fade
Or burn til final moment
With the loved ones that I've made

Connected

I have just discovered
Charles Bukowski

I came off my antidepressants
And felt a strong urge
To be re-connected with
Sylvia and Co
Amazon said I might like him
So

I showed my Balkan Boy
The poem that reminds me
Of us
Turns out he read Bukowksi
As a teenager
For the naughty bits
He said the writer was
Drunken and dirty
He actually preferred
Agatha Christie

So sweet
My wondrously
Naughty love!

Fortune's Turn

I had guessed I'd eventually land with a bump
But I hoped I'd touch down with less of a thump
It's an understatement to say I'm deflated:
My bubble is burst and I'm humiliated

All confidence shot from what's hot to what's not
And I'm lost how to find what I sudden forgot

So sweet goddess of fortune please spin your gold wheel
And help me to rise and renew and to feel
Cos I'm currently numb and feel flat and half dead
And to lose your sweet luck is to fill me with dread

A Life Less Hurried

She scared me
With her tales of doom
That shadows Would
Invade my room
That I Would Curl
Or Writhe or Wither
If new life should
Inhabit thither

And so she pressed
For barbs of wire
Or with the chemist
To conspire
To wrench your seed
From out my womb
And place it in
A tiny tomb

But I will not be
Scared by Fear
Or worried from
What I hold dear
And I will not be
Told to doubt
That anything but
Love will out

Postponing The Crone

For you e'en now
Reside in me
Your love has sown
Sweet pride in me
That I could make
Fresh life with you
And hold your hand
In pastures new
Where daily kisses
Dew our lips
And sunrise daily
Raise our hips
To dance with bliss
And glow with glee
Whatever grows
Inside of me

If new life comes
Or just our own
New joy will live
Inside our home
And thus my dreams
Will not be sullied
Of our new life
A life less hurried

The Fan of You

As I get to know the fan of you
The ever-broadening span of you
I'm moving into awe of you
As I discover more of you

At first I saw your serious side
Delighting that you didn't hide
Sincere and kind were on your sleeve
To reassure and to relieve

And then I saw you bright and young
A ready laugh and seeking fun
Then generous and weak for sweet
A trait that swept me off my feet

Consideration next revealed
(By then my fate was nearly sealed)
And just a tiny touch naive
(Your heart showed next upon your sleeve)

I knew e'en then we would embrace
Your touch, your eyes, your gorgeous face
And then I felt your luscious lips
Your hands held firm upon my hips

Postponing The Crone

And then up popped your cheeky lad
Five parts sexy, one part bad
Delicious, wayward and divine
(A recipe not unlike mine)

You led me to a secret place
Beyond the reach of time and space
And there you took my mind away
All fears and cares so we could play

And softly I am changed by you
And sweetly I am healed by you
And now I know the man of you
I am the Greatest Fan of you.

Azalea Ælfric

Dionysus And Aphrodite's Fall

Aphrodite-Dionysus is a potent mix
Good luck to the one that comes betwixt
God help the one that comes between
A love that is felt so deep and keen

As powerful as lava on its way across land
As potent as water that swift erodes the sand
As wild as the wind that swoops in flight
Are the currents and the dance of this pair in the night

So don't try to stop the lava in its flow
Don't try to freeze the water to snow
Don't try to block the wind with a wall
For none will achieve anything at all

Let the elements play out and have their storm
Let the air move the mills and the molten rocks warm
The food in the bellies of the young and the old
For this is a love story to be told

Of a man and a woman and a woman and a man
Who were brought together in a cosmic plan
And if this dance can't be danced in full
And its heat and its swell and its swirl and its pull
Be expressed by a pair deserving of love
Then there is no pattern in the heavens above
And there is no point in a life at all
For this is the sweetest, most ecstatic fall.

Shrew No More

You have tamed me
Yes it's true
I am no longer
Shakespeare's shrew

And all the things
I wouldn't do
I'm willing now
To do for you

To iron a shirt
To raise my skirt
Let go a point
Forget a hurt

And say the moon
Is my bright sun
And you can have
Your every fun

And how you did it
I don't know
I only know
I love you so

Resolve

Hold tight my Dionysus
Your ice cream time comes soon
Then I will melt upon your lips
And on your tongue I'll swoon
You can devour me inch by inch
And even eat my cone
So patient be, with some restraint,
When you are on your own

Or if it's chocolate that you want
The richness and the tingle
Then in your mouth again I'll melt
And in my mouth we'll mingle
And as I soften to your touch
You'll harden with resolve
Before my heat engulfs you too
And sweetly you'll dissolve

Whatever be your taste today
Whatever you may crave
Just wrap me in your sweet embrace
And be my willing slave
And I will follow easily
The route of your desire
And every spicy recipe
Roasts in our mutual fire

Postponing The Crone

And if I need a drink to quench
My never ending thirst
For every flavour of your skin
Then in my mouth please burst
And when we've feasted night and day
And day and night again
You'll never need a crumb of food
To take away your pain

For you will know that ecstasy
Resides within our grasp
As you plunge deep inside of me
And draw from me my gasp
My belly aches for more of you
And all our cares will cease
When we consume each other
In our very favourite feast

Azalea Ælfric

Ode to My Pubic Hair and Its Lack Thereof

I'm missing all my pubic hair
I'm wishing it was still down there
It made me feel quite snug and safe
A tufty, mufty, wholesome waif
Without it I look smooth but plump
A sad, forlorn and naked bump
And just to think it was for horn
For my new man who likes his porn
I guess that it will grow back soon
And I'll be over my fur moon
But doubtless it will wreck his mood
As he was all for Hollywood

But I must add a second verse
In which my former stance reverse

Postponing The Crone

Not for looks but stead for touch:
I like this haircut very much
As last night you dived down with glee
To lick and suck the smooth of me
And grinning pause to tell me how
You like it even better now
And after you have had your lick
I get to ride upon your prick
And then I feel us close as one
So smooth so clear and so much fun
To slide and glide and suck and play
With nothing fluffy in the way

I change my mind with fiendish might
From porn to sweet pre-Raphaelite
And stand upon an open shell
And post my feminist to hell

British

And did those hands
Come from a land divine
And now they stroll across
This body of mine

And when you speak
Direct to my Delta
In your Balkan tongue
She remembers your language

Bring me your sword and we will
Soften stone with
Sweet nectar and only you will
Draw out my song

And in this luscious
More than pleasant land
We will paint
From a palette of
Yet unmixed colours

Holiday Forecast

Watch out for a dense cover of low lying shoulds
With occasionally outbursts of heavy blame.
After a short storm of judgements
There may be a brief clearing
With periods of intense heat
But these will be followed
By more downpours of doubt leaving
Treacherous conditions.

Take care driving when the
Pervading winds of history
May throw you off course into pockets of cliché
Watch out for the unexpected fog of recent crashes.

If conditions improve it may be possible to swim
Under the clear night skies
But storms are likely to return by day.

If you forgot protective wear then be prepared
To visit a doctor to make amends on your return home.

Humble Pie

I love how I feel in your love:
Feminine in extreme
But I can struggle with the thought
Of what that seem or mean

I never have been passive
And I rarely do submit
I strive for objectivity
And pride myself in it

Like you, I loathe the gender codes
Of which we often spoke
Yet you're preserving 'Pattern'
As the natural realm of Bloke

And to the Girls you thoughtless
Give 'Emotion' as their land
As if these territories lay to claim
Inside your manly hand

Postponing The Crone

And that's the hand that strokes my back
And holds my neck so tight
And lets me find my softness
In the secrecy of the night

So how my body and my mind
And heart can integrate
To pull together all the tensions
Sitting on my plate

Or shall I just accept
That in the menu that is you
There is a lot of ham and meat
And pretty spicy stew

And if I want my sweet dessert
So pleasing to my eye
I better do the 'good girl' thing
And eat my humble pie

Azalea Ælfric

Before You Go

I want to bring my body there
I have a gift to give
I want you to deep enter in
To where our shared songs live

I want to touch your manly chest
And you caress my breast
And surf together through the waves
And ride on every crest

I want to feel the press of you
The firmness of your cock
I want you to massage my core
And secrets there unlock

I want to melt to liquid sweet
To sigh and shake and weep
And then again this time with you
And deepest hold still keep

I want to know before you go
That we can be together
And though the pause is only days
It feels like a forever

Postponing The Crone

So let me ride upon the train
Through darkness of the night
To reach your home and their unveil
Our very favourite sight:
Of bodies two, that's me and you
Locked sacred in embrace
And you will see your choice of me
And I will see your face

So please just let yourself drive on
With focus sharp and worries gone
And like a Trojan find your way
To conquer your most taxing day
And I will be your winning prize
And you can claim between my thighs
Your power, joy and ecstasy
Whatever you do want with me

For I know you are prince and king
And I know you are everything
Of universe and stars and light
So I must share one precious night
For you to fill me with your love
From devils deep to choirs above
And help us bridge the next distance
With 'toxicating sustenance

Excluded No More

I'm out with my man
And it's just as we planned
The music is good
And we're in the mood
My dress does its dance
And I grab my last chance
To be seen with my sheen
And my love so keen
And my skin still smooth
And my moves in the grooves
And I'm simply elated
To be celebrated

So I Jubilate
That I'm on a date
With my handsome mate
And we're here out late
And it cheers me up
And it fills my cup
Cos I want to be
In the human family

Birds of Paradise

There in the bathroom
The birds take flight
Exotic, colourful
Pissing and preening

I slip through and
Hide
Listening to their
Chatter and occasional
Small Screeches
And breathing in their
Aromatic fragrance

A Phoenix amongst Birds

Questions for the New Year

Will you
Won't you
Will you
Won't you
Will you give a chance?

Won't you
Will you
Won't you
Will you
Won't you come and dance?

Meet me
Greet me
Sleep in
Sweet me
Let your seed take root?

Or is this seeking
Past my
Peaking
A point already moot?

Postponing The Crone

January 2015

Azalea Ælfric

My Modern Hero

Sir Gawain battled a dragon
Sir Lancelot slew a knight
But a modern hero's challenge
Is a very different fight

He must bow to the masters of payroll
Or lose the roof from his head
He must chivalrous be in public
But primal still in bed

He must quench out his fire almost daily
But tease it back every night
He must never roar, or use sword or force
Lest he face a terrible plight

Society has him in chains
But he mustn't rattle or moan
He must stick with the boys
Suffice with his toys
Or be cast out on his own

But when he finally finds the maid
That swells his manly heart
He must learn to drop his modern role
And play his ancient part

For a life's lived once a
And it has one chance
And life is nil Without Romance

Postponing The Crone

So rise to the challenge of being meek
But lower yourself to the primal seek
Rewards will be plenty and riches sweet
For the hero who can his fear defeat

So kneel down my knight
And with your lips
Touch my hand
And caress my hips

Then stand tall again
And I shall dip
And from my shoulders
Let my silk gown slip
And I'll bow to your sword
And I'll lie so sweet
Till we turn
And you offer your riding seat
And we'll gallop off
To the land so wild
And I'll be your maid
And I'll bear your child

So boldly to the fray my love
Stand up and have your say my love
Draw forth your voice
Express your choice
And win for us today

Sweet Dreams

I dreamt that I lay down and wept
Releasing all the tears I'd kept
From marriage broken
Loss unspoken
Even to myself

And then I dreamt that I awoke
To find a tall and handsome bloke
Who questioned me
And bought me tea
To help relieve my pain

And then I dreamt that deep we talked
And through the fairy forest walked
And touched each other
Under cover
Of green and leafy glade

And then I dreamt we lay together
Breathing deep the scent of heather
Urgent seeking
Pleasure peaking
In each other's charms

Postponing The Crone

And then I dreamt we woke a tad
Wondering at what we had
Shared with each
A precious reach
That brought us closer still

And then I dreamt the fun got big
The garish shirt, the foolish wig
The party wild
The inner child
With her new sparkly friend

And now I'm truly waking up
To what lies in my golden cup
More full than 'fore
More sweet adore
But I am scared to blink

For if I wake
And find mistake
I'll lose my dream
And all that seem
And cold light rule again

The Wolves

I blame the wolves
Not for any yellow-eyed snarling
Aggression
Nor for sharp fangs of jealousy
Or salivating taste for flesh:
Those would be some other couples'
Wolves or jackals

No, I blame the wolves for their fluff.

Had not the soft fur of them been
Scattered over my kitchen surfaces
You might not have huffed
Or puffed off in smoke
And then burnt your bridges.

This side of the ravine
I have been hauled to safety by
One hundred and twenty five
Young dancing hearts
And as many wise mothers
But you, are still there,
On far side
Licking your wounds
Hungry after all

Song Interrupted

Our Love was found through song of fate
Yet you snatch back through choice not hate
And are you sure to shut your gate
Or could you not a little wait
And settle into home with me
And smile again and share more glee
And place your seed inside of me
And start a sapling family tree

You haven't even heard our odds
From scientists (those modern gods)
Who could make stakes to slight assess
Instead of your assumption-guess

For you I'd give most everything
I'd kiss you whole and wear your ring
I'd bend my knee and clean the floor
And rise and sing and sweet adore
My gorgeous man, my one true love
My lucky find: my treasure trove

At least give space to live with me
Come down and be and give with me
And I will love and hold you sweet
Caress your brow and kiss your feet
And ease your pain, make love again
And then our song be sung

Man-Hole

The sign says no entry:
I don't care for signs
I've always been partial to
Crossing the lines

I want to know if its
Left or its Right
I want to choose if
I can't or I might

There's no one more stubborn
'Bout being told
I can't just accept that
I'm just 'too old'

Til the one who tells me is
Armed with the facts
And then I might just
Accept and relax

And know that I've tried
Or still better succeeded
Till then blind assumptions
Just won't be heeded

But now I've no space and
I've work that is calling
And that in itself
Prevents me from falling

Teles-cope

If I am to breathe you out
Accept this state without a doubt
I have to trust that it is right
And let you go without a fight
To change your truth and make a plea
Or trick you back to stay with me
(I have bargained in the past to
Hold false love and bind it fast)
But are you right and is love gone
Should we be Two or Fortune's One
And is there more or is it done
For if you're right I will get gone

But how can love so sweet be pushed
Away from us and even rushed
In hardest times with heavy loads
On longest nights and icy roads
Could not one week, one month, one spring
Be waited til you force this thing
This plan of yours birthed from your head
And pattern of the stars read 'stead.

Larder Full of Love

As love is form of sustenance
You left me with a store
Of nourishing experience
With one whom I adore
Memories of days of joy
And nights of purest bliss
Hands held snug, hugs galore
And sweetest cushioned kiss
Conversations journeying
Down paths we urge explore
Ideas shared and some opposed
But always joining more

You came to me in golden shoes
And sat and we begun
You questioned me and drew me out
And gave me back the sun
The months we shared were fortunes dance
Spelt out in stars above
And now you leave I thank you for
The larder full of love

Postponing The Crone

Azalea Ælfric

ABOUT THE AUTHOR

Azalea Ælfric resides in the body of a woman near you!

She studied Poetry and Drama at the University of East Anglia, England, and enjoys the lyrics of artists such as Nina Simone, Joni Mitchell, Carole King and Kate Bush. Azalea composed a book of poetry entitled 'Maiden, Mother, Other' following the birth of her two children and her survival with entrenched post-natal depression through their early years.

Following her divorce in the summer of 2014 she discovered the heart-melting melodies and lyrics of Chloe Charles at the WOMAD festival in Wiltshire which led to the chance encounter and romance which unfolds in *Postponing The Crone*.

Three further of volumes of poetry continue on from *Postponing The Crone* and Azalea has compiled her personal favourites from the four volumes in a further volume entitled *Cut Short*.

Made in the USA
Charleston, SC
01 September 2015